I0755012

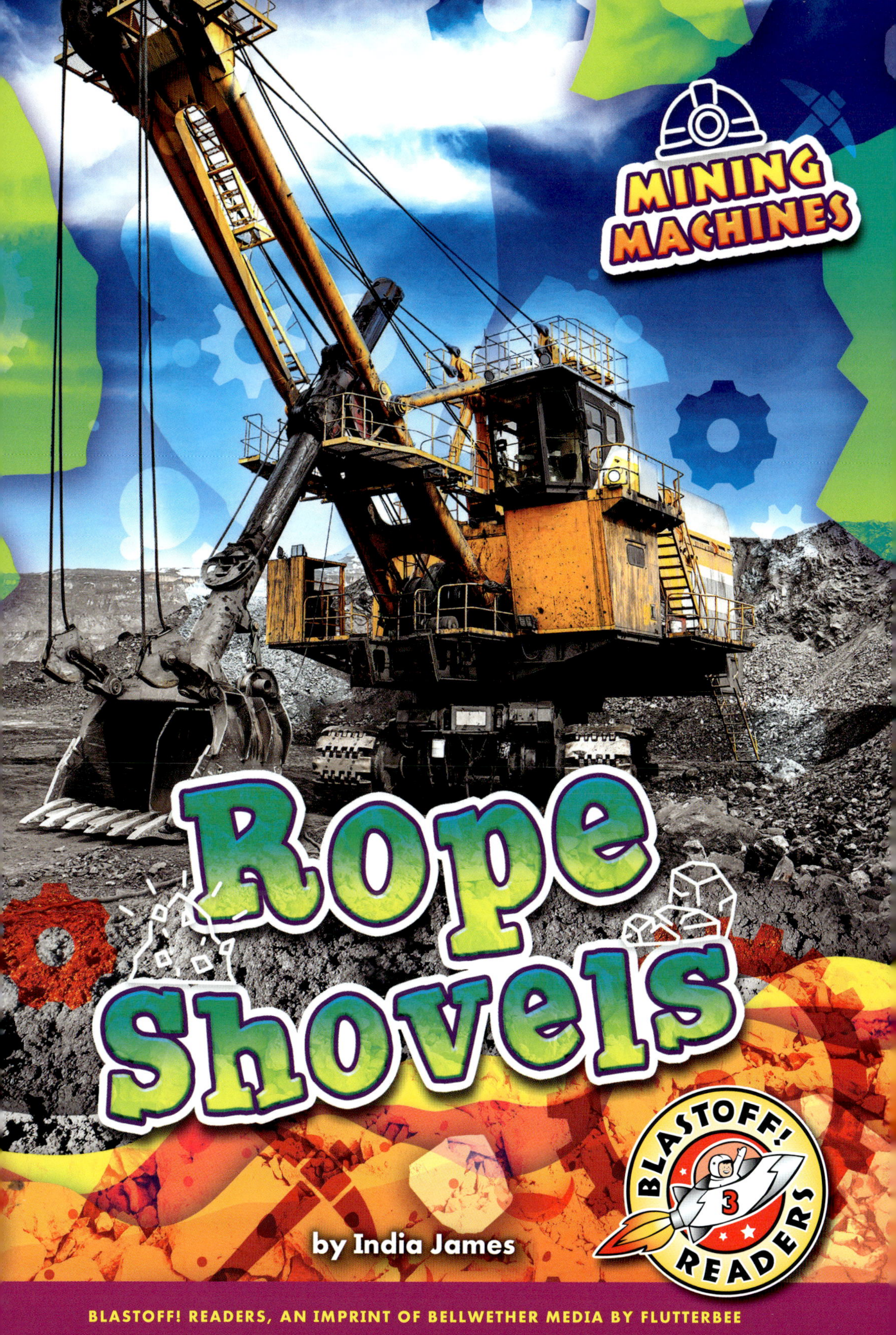
MINING MACHINES
Rope Shovels
by India James
BLASTOFF! 3 READERS
BLASTOFF! READERS, AN IMPRINT OF BELLWETHER MEDIA BY FLUTTERBEE

Blastoff! Readers are carefully developed by literacy experts to build reading stamina and move students toward fluency by combining standards-based content with developmentally appropriate text.

LEVELS

Level 1 provides the most support through repetition of high-frequency words, light text, predictable sentence patterns, and strong visual support.

Level 2 offers early readers a bit more challenge through varied sentences, increased text load, and text-supportive special features.

Level 3 advances early-fluent readers toward fluency through increased text load, less reliance on photos, advancing concepts, longer sentences, and more complex special features.

★ **Blastoff! Universe**

Reading Level

Grade K

Grades 1–3

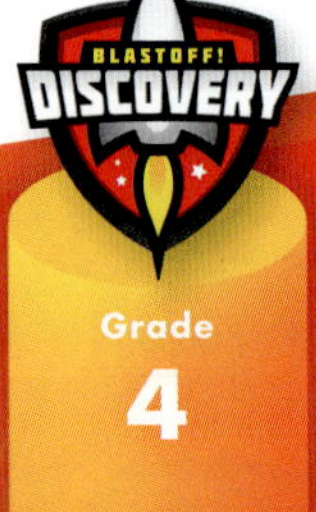

Grade 4

This edition first published in 2027 by Bellwether Media, Inc.

For information regarding permission, write to Bellwether Media, Inc., Attention: Permissions Department, 3500 American Blvd W, Suite 150, Bloomington, MN 55431.

Library of Congress Cataloging-in-Publication Data is available at www.loc.gov or upon request from the publisher.

ISBN: 9798898800727 (hardcover)
ISBN: 9798898801960 (ebook)

Editor: Kieran Downs Designer: Jeffrey Kollock

Printed in the United States of America, North Mankato, MN.

Table of Contents

What Are Rope Shovels?

Rope shovels are powerful digging machines. They are used to move dirt and **ore**.

The bucket on a rope shovel can lift heavy **loads** in one scoop.

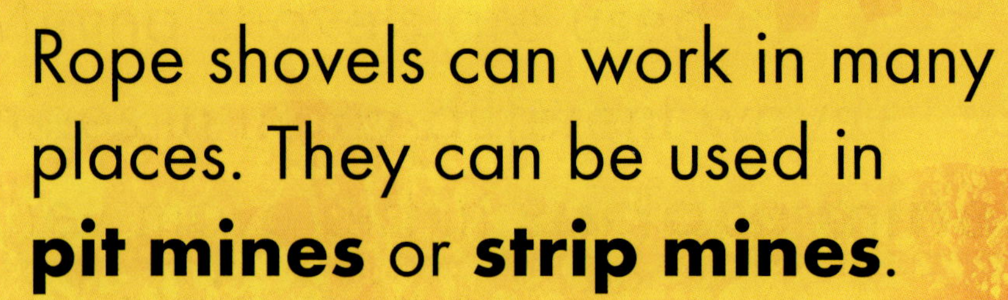

Rope shovels can work in many places. They can be used in **pit mines** or **strip mines**.

pit mine

They dig up dirt and rock.
They also dig up ore and **coal**.

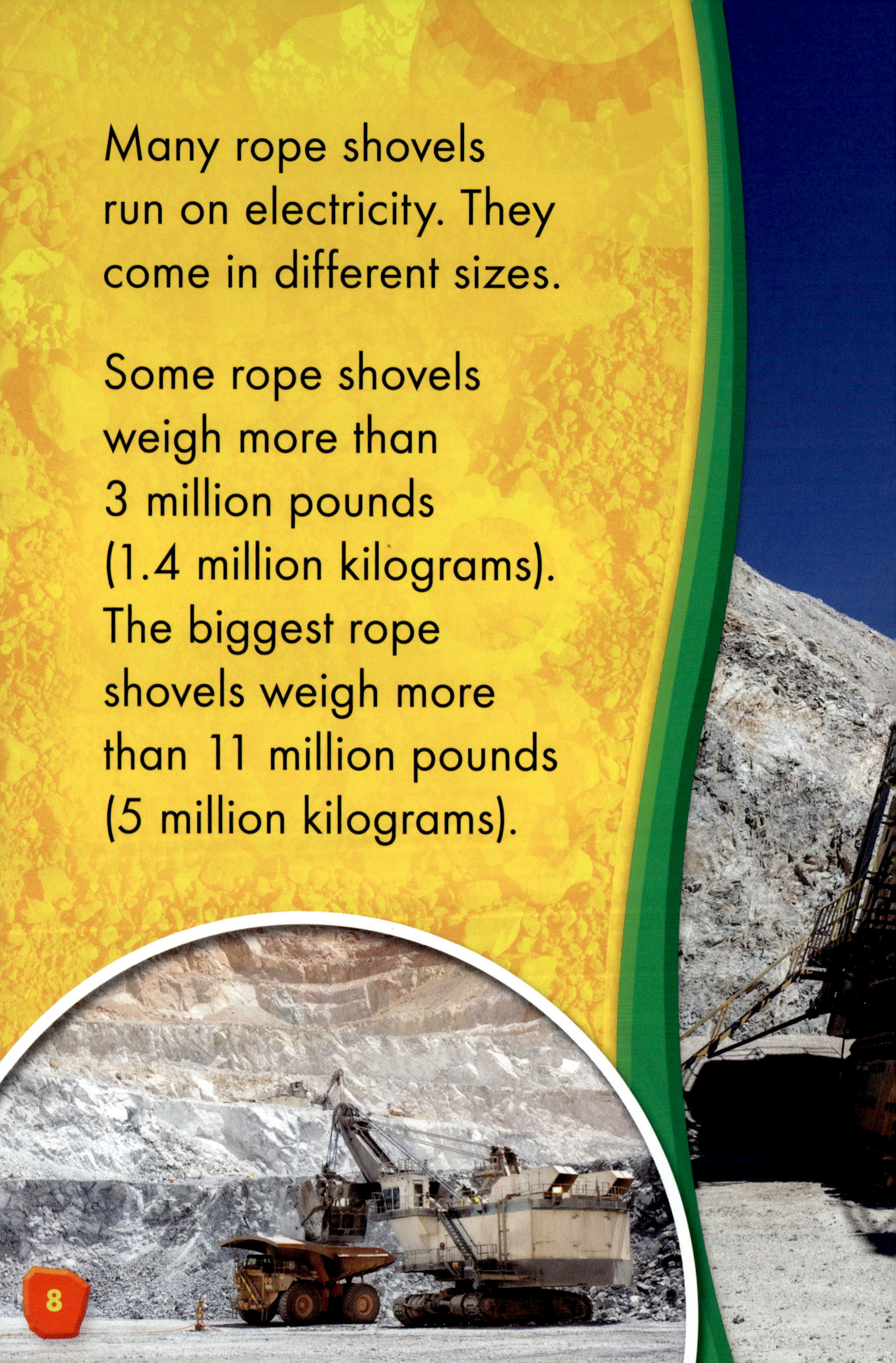

Many rope shovels run on electricity. They come in different sizes.

Some rope shovels weigh more than 3 million pounds (1.4 million kilograms). The biggest rope shovels weigh more than 11 million pounds (5 million kilograms).

XPA
2800

Parts of a Rope Shovel

Rope shovels have two long parts. The **boom** is connected to the **upper assembly**.

The **dipper handle** is connected to the bucket. It holds the bucket in place.

Ropes move the bucket. They connect to the upper assembly. They run around wheels to form **pulleys**.

Hoist ropes move the bucket up and down. **Crowd ropes** move the bucket forward and backward.

A driver sits in the **cab**. The driver controls how the rope shovel digs and moves.

Rope Shovel Parts

Rope shovels often have **tracks**. These help them move on loose or slippery ground.

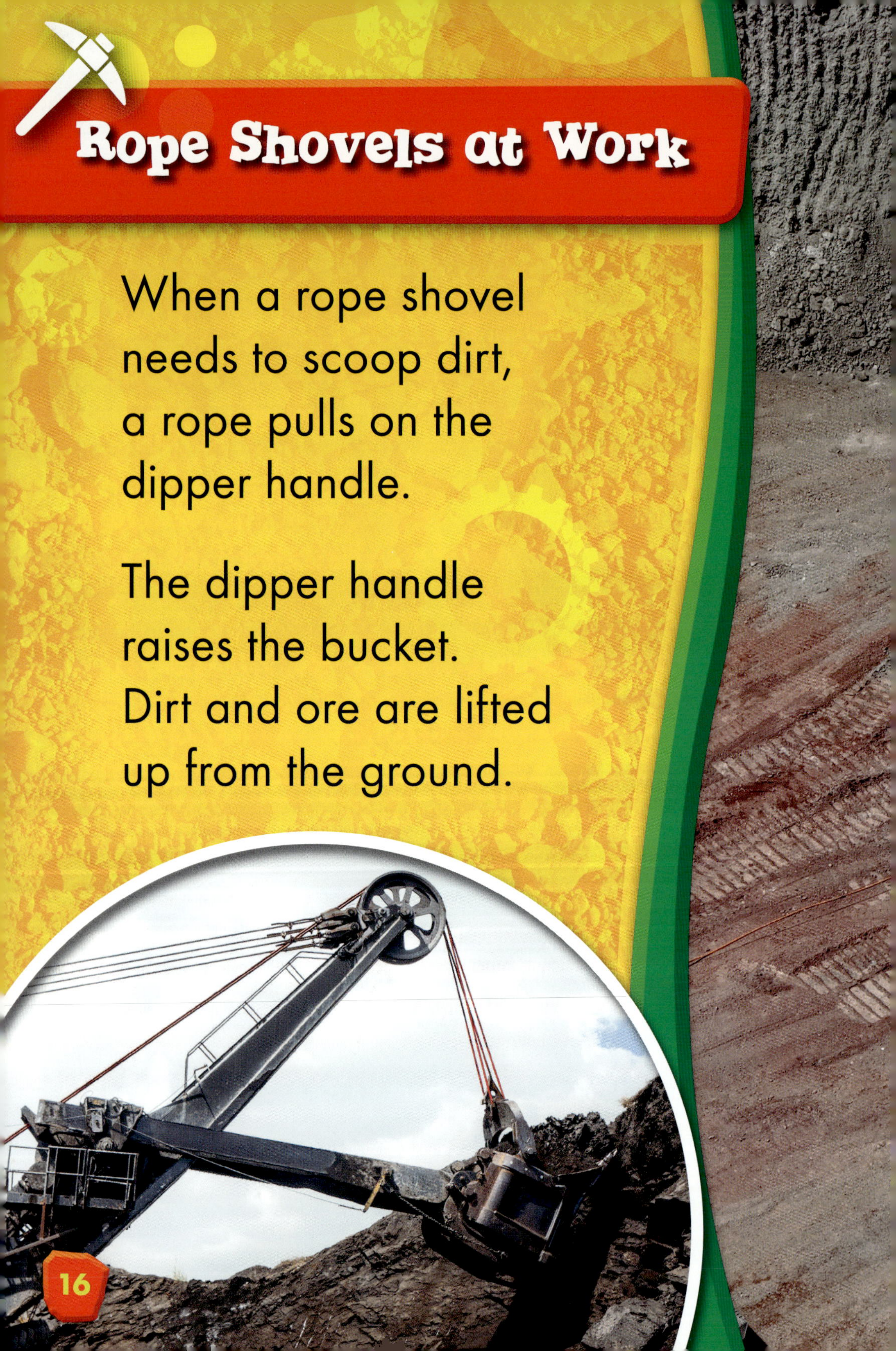

Rope Shovels at Work

When a rope shovel needs to scoop dirt, a rope pulls on the dipper handle.

The dipper handle raises the bucket. Dirt and ore are lifted up from the ground.

Rope shovels work with other machines. First, rope shovels lift dirt and ore. Then, they dump the dirt into dump trucks.

The dump trucks take the dirt away to be sorted. Ore is removed and used.

Rope shovels are powerful machines. They lift a lot of dirt and ore in one scoop.

Rope Shovel Profile

Big Brutus

weighs 11 million pounds (5 million kilograms)

bucket holds 90 cubic yards (69 cubic meters) of material

160 feet (49 meters) tall

They can also lift heavy objects like large rocks. Rope shovels are important mining machines!

Glossary

boom—a long arm on a rope shovel

cab—the part of a rope shovel where the driver sits

coal—a hard black substance that is burned for fuel

crowd ropes—parts of a rope shovel that move the bucket forward and backward

dipper handle—a long arm that attaches the bucket to a rope shovel's boom

hoist ropes—parts of a rope shovel that move the bucket up and down

loads—things being carried

ore—a valuable material that occurs naturally in the earth

pit mines—mines that get materials from deep, open holes

pulleys—simple machines that use ropes and a wheel to make lifting easier

strip mines—mines that get materials from shallow strips in the ground

tracks—parts that help a machine move across the ground

upper assembly—the area of a rope shovel that includes the cab; the rope and boom are attached to the upper assembly.

To Learn More

AT THE LIBRARY

James, India. *Mining Shovels.* Minneapolis, Minn.: Bellwether Media, 2027.

James, Ryan. *Excavators.* New York, N.Y.: Crabtree Publishing, 2025.

Rogers, Marie. *Huge Earthmovers.* New York, N.Y.: PowerKids Press, 2022.

ON THE WEB

FACTSURFER

Factsurfer.com gives you a safe, fun way to find more information.

1. Go to www.factsurfer.com.
2. Enter "rope shovel" into the search box and click 🔍.
3. Select your book cover to see a list of related content.

Index

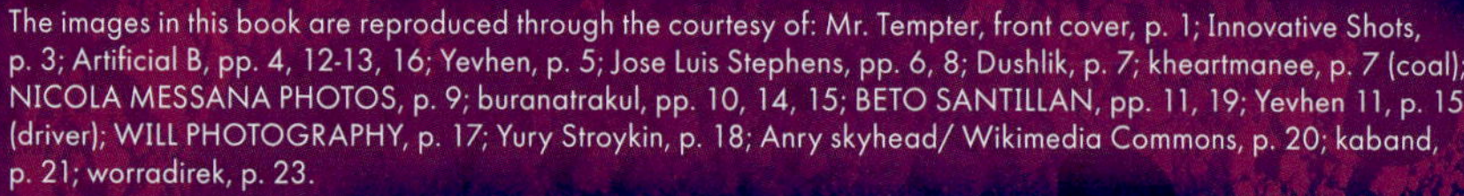
The images in this book are reproduced through the courtesy of: Mr. Tempter, front cover, p. 1; Innovative Shots, p. 3; Artificial B, pp. 4, 12-13, 16; Yevhen, p. 5; Jose Luis Stephens, pp. 6, 8; Dushlik, p. 7; kheartmanee, p. 7 (coal); NICOLA MESSANA PHOTOS, p. 9; buranatrakul, pp. 10, 14, 15; BETO SANTILLAN, pp. 11, 19; Yevhen 11, p. 15 (driver); WILL PHOTOGRAPHY, p. 17; Yury Stroykin, p. 18; Anry skyhead/ Wikimedia Commons, p. 20; kaband, p. 21; worradirek, p. 23.